SERENDIPITY

Samantha Modica

Palmetto Publishing Group, LLC
Charleston, SC

Copyright ©2016 Samantha Modica

ISBN-13: 978-1-944313-22-7
ISBN-10: 1-944313-22-2

Cover Design by: Lauren Over

For Leif

You are the brightest star on my darkest day.
Thank you for being a constant light in my life.

"Yours is the light by which my spirit's born:
— you are my sun, my moon, and all my stars."

—E.E. Cummings

PHASE 1:

BEGINNINGS

1.

The world comprises of movements.
Some movements are bigger than others.
Some feather away, almost unnoticeably,
while others weigh down decisions and outcomes.
You cannot control these movements.
If you try—and you will try—
you will embody a broken record,
                    rewinding,
to a part that neglects melody.

2.

I watch the fleeting raindrops cascade down
the windshield of my idled car.
I envy them;
for despite being unable to choose their paths,
they effortlessly navigate around one another.

Some drift away on their own,
each leaving a pattern more beautiful than the last.
Others become intertwined.
One drop drizzles into another,
forming a cluster of tranquility.

When I die,
I will be reincarnated into a thousand raindrops.

3.

Do not be afraid to love,
for love is not the poison
which comes from the liquid
enemy that sits on his bedside.
Love is what saves him.

4.

I want to live my life as a cloud,
silently floating above the ground,
waiting for the purest opportunity
to expel my lightning and pour down my rain,
ruining many days yet feeding the flora.

I want to be a necessity,
even on the days when I may not be wanted.
And silently I'll change from gray to white.
People will be mesmerized,
even though, in a matter of seconds,
I might take away the sunshine.

How powerful it would be to be so delicate
yet so destructive.

5.

I always thought of you
in the dewy morning,
when the birds chirped
rhythmically
to one another in
soprano melodies.
Though I thought of you
as the hummingbird—
quick, strategic, but
quiet as hell—
I never saw you coming.

6.

They said she was graceful
like a ballerina,
but they never knew the
chaos that built her.

7.

She saw something in the brazen horizon,
a beam of light enveloping the room through
the glare of the window.
She felt sedated by its brightness,
only able to look away when its intensity forced
tears from the corners of her irises.

But after a while the burning sensation became
comfortably bearable.
She was able to stare blankly at the Earth's bonfire,
despite their previous conflict.

It was then she realized that the longer you bear
the pain of something intended to hurt you,
the stronger you become.

She lived her life that way;
enduring pain until she was immune.

8.

The way our bodies swayed
to the melody of a broken record
was both alarming
and seemingly conventional,
for we had normalized the
scratch
skip
scratch
of that repeating rhythm
that almost no one noticed
the repetitiveness of it all.

9.

The warmth of the sun
on my skin
reminds me a lot of you
and your blazing touch.

10.

It's the way you seek shelter
between the spaces of my words
that brings about a feeling of
belongingness
to the fragments of my heart.

11.

A woman drove hesitantly down a beaten path
with her Subconscious beside her in the passenger's seat.
Trees were bare, and the road was covered with
fallen soldiers of orange, brown, and red.

Scattered intentions festered within her Subconscious'
skeleton, taunting their way to the surface of its skin.
"I know your true desires," it said.
Her subconscious leered at her from
across the center console.
"You don't know what I want!" she spat back.

Screeching from the hard jab of the breaks,
skittering across the leaves and into a side embankment,
silence lingered between them.
An unnerving difference between the present being
and her dormant aspirations.

"You will never be satisfied."

This time, her Subconscious spoke with patience.
Its voice softened, replete with understanding.
She pondered that thought long and hard.
The woman stepped outside
and calmly opened the passenger door.

She quickly yanked the specter of her Subconscious
onto the cold, wet pavement,
and she drove away.

12.

Sometimes
we long to jive
with those
whose shadows
dance only in
the dark.

13.

As I watch the sunset
beneath the willow trees,
I think to myself how
marvelous it must be
to be able to disappear
into the darkness,
only to rise again,
more beautiful than ever.

14.

She lives within the comfort of her past,
and despite how fatal it may have been,
she finds herself drawn to the chaos of it all,
unable to look forward, yet afraid of what she
might leave behind.

But the thing about the past is—
no matter how many times you try to relive it,
it will never be the same.

She knows she must stop searching for a fallen star
and start longing for the sun.

15.

Your words flowed through my body
like an electric current,
and I wondered how long it would take
for my body to give in and become
limp from your linguistic spell.

16.

She wanted to believe that he was the cosmic sun,
destined to illuminate her world,
but the closer he got, the more she realized
he was not the sun.
He was a burning meteor
headed straight for her heart,
and all she could do was wait
and brace herself for impact.

17.

I open the curtains of my window every morning
to say hello to the world.
The sun is hidden this time, though,
and not so forthcoming with her presence.
"It's okay," I whisper. "Let yourself shine."
And ever so slightly,
her rays appear from beneath the clouds,
and I'm reminded how easy it is to break free from
boundaries when you have someone there to love you.

18.

You tiptoed into my mind,
and you appeared so delicately,
so incredibly gracefully,
I never stood a chance.

19.

You can conceal your feelings for all eternity,
but I will still know
what it feels like to
be loved
by the way your dagger eyes
pierce my heart.

20.

I have surrounded myself with solitude and resentment
over the things I cannot change,
the people I cannot change,
moments even change couldn't change.
But life can throw you a rope in those elongated
and outlasted moments.

I have stumbled across a musician.
He fiddles my heart strings;
he sings melodies in my mind.

I have stumbled across a poet.
He creates sonnets and rhythm with his words,
captivating, enticing, perfected.

I want to kiss those lips,
and I want to kiss the things you say.

I am terrified of the way my heart skips several beats
anticipating you.

You,
who can cause so much light
and plausibly so much darkness.
But thankfully the most beautiful things
often come from the darkest places.

21.

My world is filled with constellations,
and you, my darling, are the Northern Star,
intent on leading me back home.

22.

The sweatshirt you gave me
no longer smells of fresh pine;
the aroma isn't of your essence anymore.
It smells like all the other garments in my closet—
familiar.

At first, the disappearance of
your enticement terrified me.
I was losing the only part of you I could touch.
An epiphany awakened me then.

I wasn't losing you.
You were becoming a part of me.
How comforting it was to become one,
unable to distinguish what's mine and what's yours.

23.

I'm afraid of falling,
but
the ground doesn't seem so far away,
and I wonder if you'll catch me,
but I kind of don't care.

Everything before has been so calculated.
I'm finally feeling out of control,
and it feels like heaven
to be able to
F
  L
    O
      A
        T
so effortlessly into bliss.

24.

This world
may seem heavy,
but if you grab
one side
and I grab
the other,
we can carry
this world
together.

25.

I've been dreaming
of the moon
and it's way of
rising every night
as a slightly
different spectacle.
And I wonder if
you see the way
that I, too, change
amongst the stars.

26.

It's always a subtle thing,
the serene ways you swoon my soul,
sacred secrets of soft silences
and spotted shadows within the smoke.
A swift sneeze, or a simple smile,
so special,
so stable.

27.

Tears trickled down my face,
so it was a water-stained mosaic,
and you whispered to me,
"You really are so beautiful."
And only then did I become art.

28.

He was perched upon the tree tops
of her forever growing meadow,
for she blossomed amongst his light,
and flourished beneath his aqua gaze.
She never went without his ivory touch,
for there was nothing she loved more
than a meadow full of flowers.

29.

And I find stability
(in this fiery life)
with you and the sun.

30.

I fall asleep gently with you by my side,
and beneath my eyelids
(in a land made only for you and I),
I envision the way we slumber on the clouds
and find comfort in the way they carry us
to the places of which we could only dream of.

PHASE II:

DISTURBANCES

31.

"It's broken!"
She picked up the remnants, and threw them forcefully.
Tiny shards propelled themselves
violently across the room,
just skimming the top of his head.

"I didn't mean to,"
he whispered shamefully.
This time, she responded calmly.
"I created a fortress for you amongst it,
and now it is shattered into splinters
that even Cupid himself could not conquer."

She exited the room.
Only fragments of her remained.
In her absence,
he tried frantically to put the pieces
of his mistakes back together;
But it was useless.
Her heart remained destroyed on his kitchen floor.

32.

I find myself searching for answers in places
where questions shouldn't be asked.
I have given many people parts of me that they
couldn't possibly take care of,
and when my affection is shattered by them—
those who I've subjectively trusted—
I will blame everybody but myself.

Is there really such thing as honesty?
Loyalty?
I, myself, locate thoughts that are deceitful
to my own moral compass.

The whispered secrets and silent chatter
fills the rooms of our distracted minds.
I have succumbed to a world that I so thoughtfully
reject and scorn.

I am no different than them,
those who I've bashed for their dishonesty.

Our lives are seas of untold secrets,
and despite our greatest efforts to escape it,
we unnoticeably surrender to the faults
which we have desperately tried to avoid.

33.

I wish you could be me for a day.
Then maybe you would understand
what it feels like to be trapped
inside yourself.

34.

Someone once told me they
didn't believe in the moon.
They thought it was just the
back of the sun.
I pitied them,
for I felt sorry they could
never appreciate the beauty
of the dark.

35.

I am stuck in the hollowness
of the spaces in between love and hate,
falling indefinitely for an undefined vow.
I am not that girl
who walks in the shadow of a man;
A man with unwarranted twists and turns,
A free-falling, mind-fucking vortex.
I am not that girl—
but sometimes we become that girl.

36.

Before you go,
I will paint you on the canvas of my mind,
so that when I reach out for your touch
and find I only capture air,
I may close my eyes and be reminded
of the serene meadows that blossomed
beneath your eyelids
and of the rose petals that flourished
upon your lips.
And I will find my peace.

37.

"What's your favorite color?"
He asked her as they stared at the dark, moonlit sky.
"Black."
He tilted his head toward her quizzically,
but she smiled with her response.

"They say that black is the absence of color,
when light just can't seem to find your eye,
and what you're left with is the visual impression
of nothingness. But I don't agree with that.
I believe black embodies everything."

"How so?"

"Because at the end of the day, when your feet
hurt from the pressure of the world weighing on
your shoulders, you stumble to the comfort of
your bed, and you turn out the light.
And in the blackness that will surround you,
you'll find everything you're looking for."

38.

I have been carefully dissecting you,
holding on to your words like shattered glass,
afraid that if I drop the pieces
they will disintegrate into tiny shards,
slicing me wide open—
an accidental display of purging red.
Ironic though,
it's a perfect depiction of our love.
You,
handing me the weapon.
Me,
delivering the pain.

39.

People say that love hurts.
That's a lie.
Love doesn't hurt.
Love is the only goddamn thing
in this world that doesn't hurt.
But people don't understand love.

The aching pit of worry in your stomach,
the feeling that flutters in suspension,
and promises to rip you open at any minute
if he doesn't call you back.

That's not love.
That's desperation.
The two are arguably so similar that almost no one
can differentiate between the two of them.

40.

You are to me
what the sun is to the moon,
distant,
but similarly bright,
and a necessity
for me to rise.

41.

I wish I could maintain the fire within me,
the burning flames that fester inside.
I cannot control them.
They take over, untamed.
I don't mean to chase you away,
but the bigger the flames get,
the more it hurts to stick around,
and I can't blame you for wanting to seek shelter.

42.

I am afraid of the sheer immensity of things.
The ocean, for instance—
filled with an abundance of the unknown.
Or how about the way you make me feel?
It has the same vastness as the ocean.

I keep wanting to throw myself in, but
I'm afraid I'll get sucked under by the tide.

I'll remain on the shore for a while,
dipping my toes in until the temperature is familiar
and I forget the dangers that live beneath the surface.

43.

I create worlds out of the creases
in my bedroom ceiling.
That is where I always find
our happily ever after.

44.

When I was younger, standing under the dewy sky
recovering from the previous night's storm,
I would collect the worms that washed up
on the cold, wet concrete.

But now I dodge the squishy creatures in disdain,
because I am running late for work.

When did life become so obsolete?

45.

She drove recklessly,
but it was diligent and purposeful.
The chaos was planned,
intentional.
She saw a police cruiser parked discreetly
on the side of the road.
She accelerates.
Zooming by, her heart raced so fast
she could hardly breathe.
He didn't follow.
It was then she realized that you can't live life
with preconceived expectations.
Nothing is ever as predictable as you might think.

46.

It's Friday night, and I'm here while you're out there.
Her presence is not hidden.
I block out the images of your hands tangled in
her hair, and I embrace the night alone.

I am not naive.
I know I'm not the only one.

It's Saturday, and it's my night.
I spend hours cocooned inside your laughter.
Your hand sweeps the stray hairs out of my eyes,
and I'll pretend, for one moment, that I belong to you.

I am not naive.
I know I'm not the only one.

It's Sunday, and I reminisce.
My hands are tightly coiled between yours and my
lips are pressed warm to your neck.
I pretend that this is my day.

But I am not naive.
I know she is your only one.
I know I will miss you someday,
but we'll be back at it again Monday.

47.

I embrace
nostalgia
only if the
memory of
you is benign.

48.

I need to believe there is more for us.
When I close my eyes, I see the last time we kissed,
and I wonder if my lips will feel this heavy forever.

I need to believe that we have more time.
I numb myself with forced smiles
until I am in the presence of myself,
and then the crushing of my chest
makes it hard to breathe
and I forget what it feels like to be whole.

49.

You stopped calling and I stopped trying.
It hurts to strain yourself, reaching for something
that will always be out of your grasp.

I never had you—
not fully.

There were moments when I was high on my tippy toes,
and a slight graze of my fingers against the softness
of your being gave me a sliver of hope.

But my calves grew weak,
and you slid away from me.

I panicked.
I jumped, and every so often I would get to you,
but as quickly as I would find your touch,
I would bounce off of you like a child on a trampoline.
I never could quite find my balance.
And so I stopped trying.

For there is nothing more dissatisfying than stumbling to my knees time and time again.

50.

I stood amongst the rising tide,
letting my toes sink beneath the sand.
I stood for a long while,
and the tide rose higher and higher,
and soon I realized that some
things are just simply out of my control.

51.

If I could go back in time
to speak wisdom to my youth,
I would whisper,
Run
as he was introduced.

52.

When the dawn has broken and the stars start to dim,
I look into your eyes and find the missing light.
Fingertips glide over my shaking lips,
trembling, afraid, misguided.

"Do you remember who I am?"

Shadows dance around my head
of long-lost memories of depleting stars.

"Do you remember all our plans?"

I felt distant and weak.
I reach out but miss, falling into a dark abyss
inside my own mind.

"I remember!"

It's too late.
He's gone,
and so am I.

53.

They say that we all come from different walks of life,
but I feel like you've been running.
And if you don't slow down and take a look around,
you might miss the sunshine that hangs brightly
above your head every single day
because you will be so clouded by the dust
kicked up in your wake.

54.

Remaining hopeful for you
is like searching for the sweetness in salt;
Useless and disappointing.

55.

She felt like magic when she was with him.
Not the kind of magic that pulls rabbits out of hats,
but the kind that cuts her in half;
leaving her body detached from itself
sending awe through the spectators.
It was the kind of magic that inspired you
to believe in anything.

But the thing about magic
is that when the curtains close
and the audience vanishes,
all you're left with is a mind full of silly tricks.

56.

There was a time
when all I ever wanted was more time,
more time to establish happiness
and leave my mark on the world.
But now—
as I stare at the revolving hands on the clock,
I wish I could stop time,
because the more time passes by,
the more removed I feel from it all.
And the faster the hands circulate,
the closer I am to the inevitable oblivion.

57.

He was the burning sun,
and she was the illuminated moon.
She always waited for him
before allowing herself to rise.
But every so often
they would dwell in the sky together,
if only for a minute.
They shared that cobalt sky
before regressing into separate entities.
That's the way it always was.
Neither would ever witness their counterpart
at the peak of their beauty.

PHASE III:

AWAKENINGS

58.

There will be days when you feel defeated.
Embrace them. For these are the days that foster
strength that otherwise may not prosper.
These are the days that inspire you
to become more than who you already are.
These are the days that matter.

59.

I don't want to be the type of person that you
comfortably know will never disappear.
I want to be the type of person
that you're afraid to lose,
the type of person that you go to bed at night
thinking about, and who you pray to God when
you wake up will still be around to help you shine.
I may easily drift, but I want you to remember
that I don't need you to feel validated,
yet I still want you to long for me when I stray.

60.

She needed to stop believing that there was
someone out there made to validate her.
She needed to stop believing that strength
and dignity came from the approval of others,
and start believing that
she is the sun
and the moon
and the stars,
and she shines brightly and independently.

61.

I find comfort in the way
the rain falls effortlessly.
For such little energy,
there is much triumph.
(Evident in the extravagant flora).

62.

The wind sounds like a thousand lions
roaring in the distance,
and I contemplate my surroundings.
The trees dance sporadically.
There's nothing melodic about their movements.
However,
I find their mayhem tranquilizing.
I become synchronized to their sways,
and soon I am aware of my heart beating
against the firm wall of my chest,
and I wonder,
has it always been this burdensome to breathe?

63.

The trees are blanketed with powdered sugar,
each flake intertwining with the last
to create intricate crystallized casings for the branches.

The snow encapsulates everything in white,
erasing the chaos from the world.
Che bella—how beautiful.

64.

I watch the raindrops collect themselves on the
lenses of my glasses until I become
distinctly aware
of the realization that nature is taking control
of my vision, and my sight becomes blurry.

It's terrifying to think about the material item
perched upon the bridge of my nose that
determines how clearly I see the world.

65.

I think of death often.
Most of the time it frightens me so much
that I become paralyzed by thought.
Other times, though,
I am comforted by the idea that there is a
resolution to all the pain and suffering.
I try to think of death not as an end,
but as a continuation of our souls,
embodied amongst those lives we have touched
who continue to walk as physical beings,
patiently waiting for their pain and suffering
to be healed by their own eternal nap.

66.

And for once, I
beckoned the rain,
for the rain had a way
of washing away
all the things that
reminded me of you.

67.

She shuffled restlessly down the sidewalk,
careful not to step on any cracks to protect
her mother from any damage.
(She was superstitious that way).

Skipping over ants and
dodging dandelions,
she reluctantly walked on her neighbors
grass to avoid the sprinklers.
She meticulously stared down at the ground,
desperately trying to keep everything in her
path intact.

Alarms blared and horns beeped.
She finally looked up for the first time
to see the chaos around her.
Imagine the impact she would have had if only
she'd gazed pleasantly ahead,
instead of always staring at the ground.

68.

She cursed herself often
by falling upon the pillow
before the sun even set.
But how could she explain
to the world that dreaming
of him was a solace better
than losing him.

69.

My heart is encapsulated in the debris of my past.
I can't shake this feeling that it's all going up in flames
and I'm going to be left with burns unable to heal.

I need you to stitch the wounds of my soul,
for all the pain and sorrows are breaking me.

I want to bloom like the flowers on my desk.
Please don't forget to water my roots.
I'm wilting.

70.

She was a child of the moon.
Her phases, too, were brief,
but she could light up the night.
(Always).

PHASE IV:

REVIVE

71.

The trees are starting to bloom,
and I wonder if you feel it too,
the way my heart's roots grow frantic
when you start to nourish them
with your waterfall eyes.

72.

If you tell me that we won't make it,
I will tell you that you're probably right.
But I would walk peacefully into the depths of our
downfall if it meant I could spend
one more night in your arms.

73.

The worst part about waking up with a heart that is full,
is knowing that at any minute the warmth that guards
your soul might disperse, and you'll be reminded
that no matter how deeply you care for another being,
you are only as strong as the reciprocity of the one who
engulfs your heart.

74.

I conceal my smiles,
for I am terrified that the world will discover too
many glimpses of my joy
and seize that power to take this feeling away.
I reserve those smiles for you—
Only
   You.
For the world has a way of taking the good
and manipulating it into something foul.
But your lips feel like the inside of a rose,
And, therefore,
I will keep you hidden in the flower pot
perched upon my windowsill
in hopes that the sun will shine bright enough
to keep this passion alive.

75.

You are
(too often)
a rolling tumbleweed,
destined for great
adventure and yet
forever a dependent
to the wind.

76.

You know the feeling all too well,
when you say so much but it never feels like enough,
when you try to encompass an entire relationship
worth of memories into a desperate plea.
How can you recap it all so abruptly?
You can't.
It comes to you in pieces in the days to come,
and you harbor each fragment of happiness
in your heart,
desperate for a way to project those trinkets of joy
into the mind of the one who has strayed.
But those memories are your own;
Don't pawn them off to a soul
who doesn't want to remember.

77.

He walked away that night
with vengeance in each step,
and she begged for his silence
because his words spewed venom.
The world never prepared her for
this type of agony.
Love is kind,
they said.
But she found nothing but cruelty
in the way he packed his bags
and left her crumbled on the sidewalk.

78.

I hate the feeling of heartbreak,
but I also love it in a self-destructive way.
Because of the heartbreak dreams
where my subconscious transforms the pain into
beautifully crafted imagery of how I hoped things
would always be.
That is where I will always keep you,
in scattered fragments on the precipice of
that infinite plane of hope.

79.

She woke up, groggy, and reached beside her,
finding nothing but empty space.
Her side of the bed was ruffled.
His was smooth, like the maid had come and
tucked everything up nicely while she slumbered
as a reminder that she was alone.
Most would feel sorrow in this moment.
She felt alive for the first time,
knowing she'd made it through another night
without him.

80.

She stared at the bottom of her glass,
wondering how she ended up there.
The man beside her had his face on
the bar counter and was snoring loudly.
The jukebox played country.
She hated country.
She lifted the glass above her head
and dropped it on the dingy floor.
The shatter woke the man up,
who then jumped from his slouch.
He grabbed her by the shoulders.
"Get out,"
He croaked.
"Get out while you can."
She ran out the door,
and then she just kept running.

81.

I find the most solid people are
always the most unreliable,
and lies told are simply shields
for our weaknesses.

82.

It is assumed that the heart can
breathe when it is given closure.
But I have learned that,
regardless of how well you handle
the end, you will always be left
wanting more.

83.

The moon has several phases,
much like we do.
I woke up one day as the black moon,
new to the darkness.
Completely covered.
Then, as slowly as the cycle goes,
I exposed my glow as a crescent to you,
holding back my brightness but
giving you a glimpse of my infinite shine.
I delivered half of myself to you
and you sat respectfully and watched as I
illuminated and our connection blossomed—
A beautiful spectacle of what was to come.
And then, when almost all of us was exposed,
we became full.
And I loved you fully until the cycle reversed
and I returned to the darkness.

PHASE V:

RENEW

84.

Please do not confuse my want for you
for a need for you,
because every time you pull the trigger
there is backlash,
and I will not be a target
for your amusement.
I desire you,
but I do not require you.

85.

My heart is an ocean of secrets,
and you are one of the darkest.
Stored beneath whispered words
and buried memories,
I swim toward the echo of our past,
and hope that I can resurface with
you by my side.

86.

Not everybody will understand our journey.
They won't see the way you gently push the
stray hairs away from my eyes when I
desperately try to hide behind my fears.
I believe the path we walk is unsafe,
but I would walk through fire if it meant
I could spend my days in heaven with you.

87.

A kiss
is simply
the collision of
atoms
creating
elements
out of
fragments
of togetherness.

88.

Desperation is beautiful.

Hiding your feelings for fear of
rejection—now that's tragic.

89.

Our passions speak volumes of us as
multifaceted human beings.
When I experience a person
speaking solely out of passion,
I become entranced
by the erratic change in their essence.
The volume of their voice
or the balanced tones of clarity.
It's as if their soul lifts from their physical being,
and I watch them dance
above the simplicity of the world below them.
How beautiful is it to witness this kind of love.

90.

When I'm dreaming of you,
are you dreaming of me too?

91.

Under the warm July sun,
I gazed at my birthday balloon.
I remember once being told,
If you love something,
set it free,
and if it comes back,
it's meant to be yours.
And so I wrote your name on that balloon,
And then I watched as it flew out of my view.
I never did see that balloon again.

92.

Positive energy seeps from you
into me,
like a sponge.
You are a waterfall,
and I am the blessed lake,
soaking up your warmth.

93.

My feet thud against the recently dewed pavement.
Next to me is a friend,
a silent lover.
He meditates amongst Mother Earth.
        Inhale.
Children play, birds chirp, and a mother
coos her fussy baby back to bliss.
E
  X
    H
      A
        L
          E
I cocoon the warmth of the sun around my body,
and I think to myself
how magnificent it is to be present in this life.

94.

I desperately
desire your
tenacity
to be able to
thrive as a
beacon
of light, even
when the day
is dark as hell.

95.

Change is fostered
by desire,
and
I am desperately
lusting for
a bump in the road
or a fluctuation in
the wind.

97.

Our lives are replete with struggles,
twists and turns,
ups and downs.
But we must search along the path
for purity and peace,
for this path awakens our souls to enlightenment
so that we may rise from the depths of darkness
with clarity, like a lotus flower.

98.

She stood silently by the river,
pondering all the luxuries the
Earth had offered her.
It was a fortunate stroke of
serendipity, the way his hand
brushed hers in that moment.
"Thank you," she whispered,
for the Earth had gifted her again.

About the Author

Hailing from a small town in Massachusetts, poet Samantha Modica has always been passionate about writing, and has written both prose and poetry. She loves to help others, which her current pursuit—a master's degree in rehabilitation counseling—reflects. Readers can also find her work on Instagram, where she writes and shares a new poem every day.

www.ingramcontent.com/pod-product-compliance
Lightning Source LLC
LaVergne TN
LVHW041215080426
835508LV00011B/969